I Forgive You

Also by Jussi Niittyviita

We Were Once Human
A Definition of Transcendence

Seeker of Silences
Contemplations of a Silent Mind

A Year of Stillness
A Journey Into Inner Peace and Awakening

7 Days of Presence
A Course in Inner Peace

The Sound of the Bells
A Story of the End of Suffering

An Inquiry Into Reality

More creations of peace and presence

available at www.jussiniittyviita.com

I Forgive You

by Jussi Niittyviita

Nothing real can be threatened. Nothing unreal exists.

Herein lies the peace of God.

\- A Course in Miracles

Contents

The Message

Beloved. I am here to bring you a message. This message will profoundly change how you perceive life. The importance of this message far exceeds anything you've ever known before. You would do well if you choose to listen to it. Perfection will dawn on you if you heed my words, and this is no exaggeration. You have my promise here and now, at the very beginning of our short joint journey, that I will not lie to you, downplay, or exaggerate the attributes or effects of the message.

The message I bring is powerful. It carries the power to transform life into ever-expanding joy and happiness. And that is what you're after, isn't it? Joy and happiness are the *only* things you seek. I know you want only them because I do too, and we're very much alike—more than you dare to think. At this point, you do not know me yet, but the empowering effect of the message will change that.

I assure you, we will become very intimate in the course of this book if you choose to trust me and listen to the message.

The message I bring holds within a secret. It is meant for your eyes only. It must remain so for the end of time and beyond. I trust you in keeping this secret because there's no other option from which to choose. This secret *is* and *can be* yours alone. Now, you might wonder what is the purpose of a secret if there is no way of telling it to others? Usually, in such situations, the purpose is lost, but not now. This time, the purpose is deep. Deeper than you can think. However, don't think any further. The message echoing here urges us to head in the same direction together. If you think too much, you will end up somewhere else than me. This is not what we want. So, please arm yourself with an open mind and a childlike attitude toward learning. This way, endless amounts of joy and happiness will follow.

The message I bring is perfect. It is like a snowflake, and it has the power to transform your experience of life into similar perfection. Heeding the message might not feel the best possible advice in some situations, but if you take my word for it now, you will eventually see the perfect symmetry and harmony the message holds within. Unveiling this promise of perfection at this point might produce some impatience in you—after all, you think you're here to find happiness, and you want it *now*. However, if I put the message in one sentence here and now, you would end up resisting it both mentally and physically. *Mentally* meaning you would judge the message downright wrong, and *physically* meaning you would throw this book away. This is not what we want. Please, be patient and listen to my words one at a time.

So, are you sincerely willing to listen? If not, then you should put this book down, and go live your life as you see fit. There are many ways to live one's life, of which none are better or worse than the others. However, you should know that all roads lead back to facing the message I bring you here. I'm holding a huge signpost to ease your efforts navigating the many roads of your life. You see, you've had quite a many aberrations which, truthfully speaking, have led you nowhere but oblivion. I am here to guide you to a road less arduous, and to lead you to a highway to where you want to be. And where do you want to be? I'm confident your destination will dawn on you as you proceed into these pages one by one.

Are you willing to listen now? Please do, for the sake of us both. Listen, and you will embark on a journey like never before. Before we begin, some words of warning are appropriate here. Do not regard this book as another trophy in your collection of '*I have read many books, and now I'm a lot smarter.*' The message I bring *is not* and *cannot* be a vehicle for intellectual arrogance. The message comes in the form of knowledge, which you may even apply in your everyday life. However, if you think knowledge and its applications are all you will gain, you have missed the point of the message. This is not what we want. You do not want to let this message slip by in the form of mere knowledge, or you will end up running blindly in circles like you've done most of your life.

*The message, when you have accepted it and understood it correctly, will show you **peace**.*

So, let us embark on this short journey together through time, where I will lead, and you will follow. When it comes to realizing the message in your everyday life, remember to be vigilant and relentless. And before all, remember to be grateful.

The Element of Harmony

At the very beginning of our journey together, I will make a statement that will startle your mind. It might not sit very well in your current experience of life, but I will say it nevertheless. I know your rational mind will find many ways to disprove the statement. You're free to follow the mind's endless logical circles, but remember that you're also free to snap out of it. The statement goes like this:

The substance of life is peace and harmony.

You are floating in an endless ocean of peace and harmony. There's only one way of not being able to see this, and that is the way of your logical and rational mind. Any chaos you encounter in the paths of your life is the product of your own mind. I will light this statement with a parable that will extend throughout our whole journey, one piece at a time. This parable also acts as a way of introducing you to the very core of the message I am here to bring.

A little soul was floating in an endless emptiness. In that emptiness, there was no content: nothing but plain infinity of emptiness. The little soul didn't know who or what it was because there was no reference point in the infinity embracing it. There was no pain or pleasure in not knowing—just a peaceful state of not knowing fluctuated within and without.

Deep in the silent shadows of the soul lingered a desire. It was not an earthly desire, but a much deeper one. This desire did not have a form or an object, for it existed in the eternal emptiness. Still, the desire was there, and the very core of it was to expand. Since there were no limits in the emptiness, there were no limits for the desire to expand either. This produced a primordial idea, which had always been, and would forever remain: the expansion would have to be within the little soul itself.

Since within and without fluctuated unlimitedly— entwined in an intimate perpetual dance—the emptiness that surrounded the little soul was present in the idea of expansion also. However, the emptiness was so subtly carrying the idea, that the little soul forgot about the emptiness, plunging deep into the idea of expansion. The little soul followed the expansion into itself.

Since you're still reading this, I feel inclined to mention that it's nice that you didn't throw the book away. There are many words in human communication that have gathered much unnecessary burden of meanings, and one of those words is 'soul'. There's no reason for you to get too religious or atheistic about it. Just treat the parable as metaphorical information. I'm sorry if I have to use words that do not always suit your rational mind, but some words carry such intense metaphorical meanings that I am inclined to use them. No better word exists to point at a primordial form of life than 'soul'.

We will return to the story of the little soul later. Now it's time to investigate the first hints of the message I bring. So, what do you think about the little soul's desire to expand? Can you feel affection toward it? Are you curious to know what it means to expand in the first place? The curiosity arises in you because you bear exactly the same desire within. The desire to expand is the very basis of human nature, and it breathes within me as it breathes within you.

This book is not about exercising any belief system or technique, but let me walk you through a straightforward guidance, which we will keep as short as possible. The guidance goes like this: *First, expand your awareness toward the world around you. Just acknowledge that there is a world which you perceive at this very moment—you might be in a room, or open space, or wherever you are. Any place will do. Pay no attention to any specific thing in that world. Then, without thought, become aware how the world is included in you.* This is how simple it is to expand. Since you can expand yourself like this, it means you *already have expanded yourself* like this without knowing it. This isn't new to you. Expanding into the world is as natural as it gets for you.

Your desire to expand might express itself in many different ways. You hope for life more satisfying and peaceful. Avoiding suffering and seeking happiness are your primary drivers, and you aspire to find captivating meanings in everything you do. These things are all unconscious expressions of your desire to expand *yourself*. Despite being unconscious expressions, there's nothing wrong with them. However, wouldn't you feel more aligned with yourself if you expanded into all those different things *consciously*? They are not ideas of you achieving or becoming something, but ideas of *you being* something. The whole world points at you because of the simple circumstance that you have expanded into the whole world.

Now let me stop for just a little moment. What I just said might reveal some resistance in you. I will repeat myself here to make the point clear enough:

You have expanded into the whole world.

I hope I didn't lose your rational mind saying this. An urge might arise in you to put the book down and label it as spiritual mumbo-jumbo, but please, just bear with me. It will very soon dawn on you that the message I bring is neither philosophical or spiritual. Labeling anything as 'spiritual' is just a product of your rational mind. There is nothing spiritual in the world. There is no particular place or time to be spiritual. Being spiritual is not something you can turn on and off. I might only use the word sometimes to point out some subtle truths in a way you have learned to understand.

Together we're limited by the human vocabulary that can only go around in circles—defining one word through other words. Language is like the snake Ouroboros eating its tail, yet here and now, language is what I must use to communicate the message to you. In other words, to catch a fish, you must place the hook under the water. This is why this book exists in the first place—to guide you out from the deep waters of the world you've learned to live in. So, treat me as a fisherman, who will lift you above the surface and show you an entirely different world than you've ever known. But unlike fishermen usually do, I will set you free at the same instant you've seen my world. Wherever you will then expand is your own choice. It has always been, and it will always be so.

The most crucial aspects of your expansion are forms that seem to reflect yourself—other human beings, whom I will refer to in the future as your 'brothers and sisters'. With them, you seek familiarity, peace, and harmony. But with them, you might find yourself in the most grievous situations ever. Relationships—both intimate and casual—withhold inescapable gravity from which you cannot hide. This gravity is your doorway to joy and happiness. I'm not saying it is the only doorway, but it is the one you have attached most meanings to.

I must mention at this point that the doorway is not actually a doorway since there is no door to joy and happiness. They are intrinsic attributes of the life that you express by simply being human. Therefore, many mystics throughout eons have referred to this as the doorless door, the gateless gate, which one must pass to find true joy and happiness. It is a portal without frames, and when you pass through, everything around you stays seemingly the same. There's a saying in one of your perennial philosophies: *before enlightenment, life is carrying water and chopping wood, and after enlightenment, life is carrying water and chopping wood.* Only your perception of everything has shifted toward something that you call joy and happiness. And to make it even more clear, changing your perception doesn't mean you have changed. It just means you have become aware of joy and happiness into which you have already expanded.

This discovery of joy and happiness sounds easy, doesn't it? However, if it were easy, you would have found lasting joy and happiness long ago, along with billions of your brothers and sisters. Here's where you go off track: you believe the world is supposed to make you happy. If that were true, you would already be full of happiness, and most probably wouldn't be reading this book. You must trust me when I say that the world doesn't owe you anything—the world is not responsible for your happiness.

The world doesn't need to change for you to find happiness.

When you realize that neither the world or you need to change to discover joy and happiness, you will begin to see peace and harmony around you. *Everything* entwines peacefully in the same intimate dance of the little soul. This intimacy is found most clearly in human relationships, into which we have all expanded. In those relationships, there are many 'elements of harmony'— both named and nameless ones. I am here to bring the message of the brightest of them to you.

We call this element of harmony *forgiveness*.

Introduction on Forgiveness

What do you think forgiveness is? *First*, I would have you understand that forgiveness is not what you think it is. It cannot be what you think it is. Otherwise, you would already naturally express forgiveness. There are many things other than forgiveness that I must clarify before you're able to understand forgiveness. *Second*, I need you to be sincere if you want to find out what forgiveness is. Without sincerity, you will end up finding nothing of real value. *Third*, you must know that I forgive you. Despite everything you've done to me, I forgive you. But don't get me wrong—you have not done me *wrong*. That would be impossible.

Now, you might ask why on Earth do I need to forgive you? We barely know each other! It is much too soon to answer this question, but I promise that until the end of this book, I will provide you with an answer. For now, just rest assured that you have been entirely and unconditionally forgiven. I know that on some level, it feels nice to be forgiven, but I do not forgive you because you need my forgiveness. I forgive you because I need to forgive.

Here's a perfect time to wander back to the parable of the little soul for a while. Remember how she expanded into herself, reaching ever further and deeper while floating in the infinite emptiness? Now she does something remarkable.

At first, it was impossible to tell if the expansion was fast or slow since there was no concept of time involved. The little soul felt joy within. The joy knew no boundaries, and it expanded into the very core of the little soul, merging with the emptiness in which it existed. The little soul had always known what joy was but had never experienced it—not before now.

As joy was made manifest, so too did the concepts of before and after. The desire to expand was initially formless and without content, and where there was no form or content, the idea of time could not exist. As joy appeared, it created content for the desire. With the desire being fulfilled, an endless yet very subtle joy followed wherever the expansion proceeded.

The little soul moved and reached for the furthest part of itself, and saw this part as a reflection of itself. Now there were two separate reflections within the little soul experiencing one another, yet they were fundamentally one. However, as the little soul perceived itself through the reflections, the sense of oneness disappeared, and a sense of separation emerged.

The little soul observed the reflections of itself, and a question arose: "Who are you?" Simultaneously, without the smallest gap in time, another question emerged: "Who am I?" The questions expanded into both reflections at the same time. The formless power of the questions seeped into the unseen emptiness in which they silently echoed.

The miracle of existence is the most mysterious thing known to the human mind, and if you're honest with yourself, the second mysterious thing to wonder is the question: "Who am I?" There's no other question that can even compete with the peculiar power of this one. This statement applies only if you're sincerely honest with yourself. I know you think that there are many more important things on which to contemplate in this world. You might think that "Who am I?" is a question reserved for spiritual growth and secret societies of enlightened gurus, that have no real connection to the mental, physical, and economic growth of *you* and the real world in which you have to live.

As I promised at the beginning of this book: I will not lie to you, downplay nor exaggerate the attributes or effects of the message I am here to bring. So, please trust me when I say that no more important question exists in the world for you to ask than "Who am I?". The choice is now and always yours, and there's a vast collection of questions from which to choose. All I ask is that you choose wisely.

Let me elaborate this a bit more, to make it easier for you to understand. If nothing else was true about this world, there is definitely some form of existence conscious of your life—let us decide together here and now that this form of existence is *you*. Otherwise, *your* life would not exist. Don't get drawn into the new age ideas that we might not even exist at all, or this is all just a giant simulation, or whatever theories you've gathered in the past. Again, if you're true to yourself, there is undoubtedly someone or something aware of your surroundings right at this moment—someone who is holding this book in their hands. Someone who has a sense of residing in the body with all the curious senses it bestows—there are smells, sights, sounds, and a variety of sensations if you're but willing to see and listen. Who is it that is aware of all this? There's someone who has dreams, who has something to achieve. Someone who loves whatever you love and hates whatever you hate. Who is it *here and now* that has or wants something? Who is it?

Remember what the little soul asked? "Who are you?" Remember what the little soul's reflection asked at the same instant? "Who am I?" If the silent teaching echoing in this part of the parable did not yet dawn upon you, I assure you it will at the latest when you turn the last page of this book. If you understand this teaching intellectually, but cannot *experience* it when dealing with your brothers and sisters—who are reflections of yourself—then you might be thinking too hard. Don't be too hard on yourself, and the experience will emerge by itself. On the other hand, if you do understand this teaching intellectually *and* can also experience it, you most probably know everything there is to know about forgiveness. In this case, there's probably no other reason for you to continue reading this book but the joy of doing so.

Contemplate this teaching. Spend time with the question "Who am I?" and do not settle for already existing answers. Especially, do not settle for any answers that arise as words or mental images—such answers will beget only ignorance. Spend so much time investigating the question that your ignorance shifts to self-gained knowledge, and knowledge shifts to experience. You might find it difficult, but only because your intellectually arrogant mind tells you it is difficult. It doesn't tell you that directly, but sneaks in through the backdoor of your consciousness, creating many other things to think about. The mind offers you things that are seemingly more important. Just trust me when I say that it is your essential nature to wonder Who You Are, and don't let anything undermine that state of wonder.

Let's backtrack a little. A few pages ago, I scratched the topic of the miracle of existence. Miracles connect so intimately to *forgiveness* that we must not let them slip by without some more investigation. The world deserves miracles, wouldn't you say? Miracles make life worth living. Miracles lift your spirit sky-high as you witness them with gratitude. But they are not what you usually regard as miracles. True miracles are not planned. They are not conscious deeds. They are not the magnificent anomalies you witness in the world once in a while. Miracles are a natural unfolding of the world where there are no judgments based on the ego, conflicts, and confusion. True miracle is a paradigm shift in the human mind. We will dive deeper into the concept of the 'the ego' a bit later on our journey because on the path you're walking, understanding the ego is crucial in every way.

Everyone is entitled to miracles, including you. This is because the very essence of your being breathes the substance of miracles—peace and harmony. You are their source, and because of this simple truth, there is no order of difficulty among miracles for you. There are no bigger and smaller miracles, nor are there harder or easier miracles. Miracles have an innate power for healing. Whenever you feel inner peace and your normal state of silent psychological suffering ceases to be even for a fraction of a second, you become an expression of true miracles. 'A Course in Miracles' is a book to be cited here because the same message that I'm here to bring to you, also echoes in the pages of that book:

*"Miracles are natural. Whenever they do **not** occur, something has gone wrong."*

Now, the part of your mind where the intellectual arrogance and the ego reside might cling to the subject of the abovementioned suffering. "Your normal state of silent psychological suffering, you say!? I do *not* suffer! My life is good. And also, miracles are not at all what you say they are! There are bigger and smaller miracles, and we all must strive to achieve such things!" If something like this just arose within you, I assure you are suffering—silently, as I said. Silent suffering means that you don't even notice it yourself. In the state of silent suffering, when you do *not* perceive yourself and the world full of miracles, then "something has gone wrong," and this is not what we want. We are here to fix this together.

Please, remember this from here on: judge not yourself for your own words and thoughts, but if you do, forgive yourself for judging. The forgiveness must be immediate to prevent the effects of false judgment take any form of action. Therefore, forgive before you act and witness miracles.

The book you're holding in your hands is not just a book. It is my promise to you that you have already been forgiven. This promise leads us to *the angle of reentry*—the perspective from which we will investigate the element of harmony called forgiveness. Just to make sure that my choice of words did not confuse you, I will shed light on this 'angle of reentry' in a way you're familiar with. When a spacecraft approaches Earth, there is a massive risk of bouncing off the atmosphere if the angle of approach is not perfect. Even minor calculation errors might produce critical outcomes, so accurate navigation is everything when reentering Earth's atmosphere.

Now, imagine you're in a spacecraft that is returning to home from afar. You, and only you, are responsible for safe landing to your beautiful home planet. To ensure that you don't bounce violently back to space, or burn to cinders while approaching too fast, you must press all the correct buttons and pull all the right levers. You really must know how to operate the spacecraft, and in addition to that, you must know every single detail of the whole landing process. In this process, the angle of reentry is one of the most crucial aspects. Yet all the knowledge you have about your spacecraft and the process of landing is not nearly enough. You must also be aware of what is happening every single moment. You have to be aware of the situation, as well as yourself. Without complete awareness, your ride will end up quite a rough one. This is not what you want.

You want to return home safely, so you can experience the unique grandeur of all the small things your home planet bestows. It offers you some clean air to breathe, fresh water to drink, gravity that keeps everything in place, diversity of nature everywhere you look, and other commonly unnoticeable things that you easily take for granted. Most of all, you want to return home to your loved ones and the relationships that await your presence upon your arrival. Being able to experience all this once again depends on your angle of reentry.

Let's get down to Earth from this analogy. Even though the spacecraft analogy explains our angle of reentry in a concise way, forgiveness is not rocket science. It does not involve intellectual contemplation. You will go downright wrong, bouncing back to the dark space from where you came, if you involve intellectual arrogance with the angle of reentry. Now that we have covered the subject in layman's terms, it is time to reveal the angle of reentry:

No one in your world ever needs to be forgiven,
but you are always the one who needs to forgive.

The reason I used the spacecraft analogy is that you have forgotten your innate ability to forgive. You are not navigating accurately enough back home, although home is where you want to return the most. Here and now, reentry means remembrance, which will lead you back home. And to remember, there must be something triggering your remembrance because it rarely happens by itself. From here onwards, I will call these triggers *the points of entry*.

The Points of Entry

et us start investigating the points of entry with a simple analogy. I choose this approach here mainly because human life—the very life that you also are—is one vast point of entry into elements of harmony, including forgiveness. Imagine a small pond with fresh immovable water, whose surface is still and clear like a mirror. Everything in that pond breathes life in a very subtle, yet distinct way, and the beautiful surface conceals mysteries deeper than you can imagine.

Then it starts to rain. The first drop of water falls from the clouds on the still surface of the water, and the beautiful dance of wave-like motion begins. The impact of the waterdrop creates waves of different magnitudes that expand evenly in every direction. Then a second drop falls, breaking the stillness of the pond's surface even more. The waves interfere with each other, and a hint of complexity is introduced to their delicate dance. A third drop falls. The complexity of the waves' interference increases even more. Then the whole of heaven starts pouring down. The surface of the pond is now full of little impacts, each creating their waves, interfering with all the other waves. The impacts of the falling waterdrops are very quick as you observe them—they appear in a blink of an eye, and in the next moment, they are already gone. The waterdrops merge with the pond, and afterward, all that is left is the waves.

Human lives are such impacts on the surface of the pond. Just like the impacts appear and disappear in almost at the same instant, so do you also. Your life is but a tiny splash of water in a small pond. I do not mean to undervalue your life saying this, and there's no space to be pessimistic here either. Let me clarify a little the core lessons of this pond-analogy. There are two lessons here: *the lesson of the source* and *the lesson of unity*.

I will not go very deeply into *the lesson of the source* while bringing you the message echoing in these pages. This is because the source is practically impossible to convey in words. All the words in the world can only point to the general direction of the source, and going consciously in that direction is not our common interest here and now. So, you have to settle for just one sentence concerning *the lesson of the source*. To be as clear as possible I will clothe the sentence in the words of our pond-analogy:

All the waterdrops fall from the same sky into the same pond.

Now, we will investigate *the lesson of unity* a bit more thoroughly, since it benefits our common quest of me delivering the message and you listening to the message. We will dive into it shortly at this point, and when we arrive at the very end of this book, we will get back to *the lesson of unity* in more detail.

The cornerstone of *the lesson of unity* is to realize that all the waves exist in the same pond. All the interference of those waves happens in the same pond. There is no way out for them, so every single wave created by every single waterdrop contributes to the big picture in the same way. Together, all the waterdrops are equivalent, no matter how big or small they seem—and every single one of them fulfills the interference pattern of the waves.

So, we're tiny splashes in the same pond. How come you don't feel that way, you might ask? I will elaborate on your question in a more definite form: why does this distinct sense of separation occur? To understand *the lesson of unity*, you must first understand the sense of separation. What I mean by 'separation' is nothing spiritual here. The sense of separation is just what happens when you take a look around—you notice that you are a separate individual from the surrounding world. For example, you feel other human beings are someone else than you, and the clouds in the sky seem very far away, and all the objects in the room bear relationships to one another that is governed by the distance in between them. So, everything just feels simply separated.

Now here comes a spoiler of the message, and if you can *know* and *experience* the following, there will be no more reasons to continue reading this book, other than just the joy of doing so. *You* are the one that creates this peculiar sense of separation, and you do it for one reason only: you're afraid of *the lesson of unity*. Let me put it into even more understandable terms here because this is highly important. The following will most likely upset your rationally thinking mind:

All your life, you have been afraid of yourself.

Since the first signs of your identity emerged during your early time here, you have been increasingly afraid of yourself. You might not feel that way because you find false solace in the many things within the separation you have created yourself. But the separation is only an idea, an armor you have created to protect yourself from your own creations. What you don't see is that the armor that's supposed to protect you is actually hurting you and causing you very much unnecessary suffering.

The lesson of unity exists only to dismantle the illusion of the armor you've created. That is its sole purpose. Only when you can see your dull armor in the shining state of acceptance and love for yourself, will *the lesson of unity* be fulfilled. If you refuse to accept that you're afraid of yourself, the refusal emerges because of this same armor, and in the state of refusal, you will continue to be afraid of yourself. You don't even see it happening—the armor itself is invisible, yet it affects your life in every possible way. I humbly ask for your trust at this point when I say that *the lesson of unity* is what will eventually set you free. When you realize this lesson, all the elements of harmony, including forgiveness, will blossom infinitely and without limits. However, it's too soon to discuss *the lesson of unity* here further. We must first go through a few other things to prepare your understanding. These things are *the points of entry*.

So, let's jump back to our spacecraft for a little while now. When approaching Earth in a spacecraft, you must first go through the atmosphere to make your way to the surface of the planet. After landing, the atmosphere is still there, but what gives you the feeling of home is the surface. Similarly, there are two points of entry when talking about elements of harmony: one is the outer world, and the other is the inner world.

The outer world is what you experience through your perceptions, and the inner world is the one you mostly live in. These two worlds relate to one another in size just like the atmosphere relates to the solid planet under your feet. In your normal state of consciousness, when engulfed by the makings of the human mind, the inner world outweighs the size of the outer world just as massively as the planet outweighs the atmosphere.

Both of these worlds are important for you to have what you call experiences. However, the problem with the human mind—which you and I both express—is the imbalance between these worlds. You gravitate toward the inner world so intensely that you lose awareness of the outer world. In other words, you take the atmosphere for granted and breathe through the gravitational effects of your confused state of mind. This statement brings us to one of the most important teachings this book holds within:

Whenever you forget any part of yourself, you forget yourself.

Remember this when you emerge through your present state of oblivion. A true answer to the question "Who am I?" will inevitably arise, and when it happens that you truly know yourself, *do not forget yourself.* Never again forget yourself. Never forget even the tiniest part of who you are because if you do, you will forget yourself entirely—again. This is not what we want. This is why I'm bringing you the message echoing in these pages.

Now that I have established the two separate points of entry, I must clarify that I've separated them only because of teaching purposes, to make understanding occur through the divisive nature of your mind. Your mind can only know separation. In truth, there are no separate inner and outer worlds with you. There's only one world that exists, only one ecosystem called Earth floating in an empty space, and only one existence which happens in itself. But as I said a bit earlier, you can treat me as a fisherman here, who will lift you above the surface so you can see more clearly what has always been there. I must do the lifting using words and techniques understandable for your mind. Hence, the separation of the two points of entry.

We've gone some distance without the parable of the little soul. Now it's time to get back to her. I must mention that the little soul could just as well be a 'he', but using the ancient mythical aspects of our species' history, I've decided to call the little soul a 'she'. This is because she's doing some heavy creation work of which the males in human societies are seemingly incapable.

The two reflections of the little soul danced in the emptiness, wondering the perpetual mystery of one another with compassion and gratitude. The mystery was deep, and even though the reflections were distinctly perceived, the silent mystery that created the reflections could not be unraveled—it was not possible through their forms. The little soul had started to forget about the mystery of the emptiness that encompassed the forms. Only forms existed for the little soul.

The little soul created more and more forms that could only be defined through all the other forms, and never solely through themselves. Relative existence started taking shape. As the complexity of that existence deepened, so did the mystery underlying the existence grow dimmer. Eventually, the myriad forms created such vast patterns of immense complexity, that the little soul forgot everything else.

As the mystery of existence disappeared into clouds of oblivion, the primordial wonder, compassion, and gratitude followed into the veil of the same clouds. But they were not entirely lost, for the little soul was still essentially the foundation of the existence of all forms. The little soul only could not remember it. Those basic elements of relative existence could not be entirely lost because they were floating in the same eternity that still fluctuated within and without, never beginning or ending.

Symbols of wonder, compassion, and gratitude remained in existence, even though their reality was forgotten. Out of those symbols, the elements of harmony were forged. Harmony started spreading throughout the little soul's body of creations. Subtly and almost unnoticeably, the harmony aligned the existence into accord with the prevailing, yet silent mystery of it all.

With the invisible wings of harmony, the little soul approached the sense of separation that governed the countless forms in existence. It became obvious that the separation was not a product of distance or time between forms, but a symbol of the little soul's primordial idea of expansion. In each of the forms that seemed separate from one another, experiences of an outer and inner world emerged. It became evident that those seemingly separate worlds would act as the points of entry to the home that the little soul had forgot about. The bridge that would connect the points of entry to the home was an element of harmony called forgiveness.

As forgiveness was discovered, the mystery whose whispers echoed in every corner of existence started slowly emerging once again through all forms. The little soul's work of true creation and expansion through relative time and space had only just begun.

I hope I didn't confuse you with this part of the little soul's expansion. I expressed it as clearly as is possible through words. You must have realized by now that words are a highly limited form of expression, that will only go around in circles at best. Remember the snake Ouroboros eating its own tail? You might not have realized yet that when you think with words, you separate yourself from your surroundings—from the world that is a step closer to what we could call the reality. But we're going to change that here and now.

Your return home is our common interest, and from the hallway of our home, I invite you to step in. However, you cannot step in carrying your normal state of conditioned compulsive thinking. You cannot step in with your burdens of the past, or your expectations of the future. There are many things you must cease doing here and now so we can proceed in fulfilling our common interest.

Stop analyzing.
Stop giving meanings.
Stop creating stories.
Stop labeling things.
Stop judging.
Stop comparing.
Stop thinking.

I will leave a blank section here just to emphasize how important it is for you just to stop.

Now, are you stopped? Are you really stopped? You can still read this book because hearing the message does not require any complex intellectual analyzing through thinking. Your mind might continue with its incessant chatter, but I'm asking, are *you* really stopped right now? If you are, your mind will follow you to the inner silence eventually. If you're not, then the simplest way to do this is to detach yourself from the makings of your mind and *remember* how it feels just to *be*. Don't use any force in doing this because exercising force will only become another illusion of your mind. Just let everything—and I really mean *everything*—be just the way it is, including your seemingly precious thoughts and emotions. You need only be still.

The reason I just used the word *remember* above needs some elaboration at this point. If you find that being still is difficult, and the mind starts raging about myriad things after a painfully short inner silence, it means you've identified with the forms of the mind too deeply. The little soul in you has become entangled in the many forms within your perception. Being still and silent is not difficult in any way—it is your birthright here and now, and forevermore. Please, trust me when I say that inner peace is what you essentially are. The reason you haven't experienced inner peace up to this moment is that you've been afraid of yourself. Everything added to the state of stillness and inner peace is either insane or delusional, many times both. You have never lost your inner peace, and it shines through you with a bright light eternally. Time cannot touch what is eternal, nor can you ultimately deny it. Inner peace and simply *being* is who you are. You just need to remember yourself.

Now, this is one of the greatest turning points on our journey together. From here onwards, you must harbor an intention to remember who you are. The intention must be there because it will be your lighthouse guiding you back home. It doesn't matter if you don't remember who you are yet, but the sincere intention to remember makes all the difference. If you cannot commit to this intention, I advise you to put this book down and let time happen to you. I assure you, time will give you suffering. When you have suffered enough, you will find the message again, and you will be ready to accept the humble intention to remember who you are. However, taking the long and arduous road is not what we want here, so I hope you strive to find the intention to remember who you are—which is essentially inner peace and primordial *beingness*.

Be very careful not to take the egoistic path here because the danger of doing so is very evident. The ego wants to achieve something by creating a false sense of intention. If you're not sincere with your intention in finding who you are, you will end up chasing ghosts that do not even exist. To make this danger less abstract, I will give you a piece of practical advice, whose importance I cannot underline enough with words:

As I said earlier, time cannot touch what is eternal. Time and eternity exclude one another—time has nothing to do with eternity. The past or future has nothing to do with *you*. Any preconceived ideas about the present moment have nothing to do with you. Time is the realm of the ego, and you don't want to take any part in it because of the simple fact that neither the ego or time exists. If you give life to them, you simultaneously exclude eternity from your reality. This is not what we want.

Despite this grave danger of chasing the non-existent, you cannot be totally lost. What is eternal cannot be lost, but only forgotten. And even the state of oblivion cannot last for very long because the elements of harmony were devised *for* you. These elements will regain your sense of primordial wonder, compassion, and gratitude, and the bridge that will take you back home from the confusion of time is *forgiveness*.

Now, I'm truly grateful if you found and accepted the intention to remember who you are. Otherwise, you would be afraid of all this talk about eternity. Just to make sure you're on the right track, let's clarify one thing: if you found yourself doubting or rationalizing the eternity-talk here, you obviously did *not* understand what I just advised a few pages ago. You did not stop thinking. The simple act of thinking is prone to close the doors of true understanding. And because you were thinking, the intention to find yourself was really not there. I advise you once again to find the intention here and now, or put this book aside and let time happen to you first.

So, let's continue on our journey's next important phase. Just like in the parable of the little soul, the *points of entry* need to be established. The *points of entry* are basic forms that, when you learn to perceive them in the correct way, will guide you back home. Now that you're in the hallway of our home—devoid of the confusion of time, detached from the compulsive conditioned thinking, and armed with the sincere intention to find who you are—I invite you to step closer. I invite you to investigate the sense of separation you witness everywhere you look. This is because when you become aware of who you are *not*, you will begin to realize who you are. The next phases of our journey are about getting rid of obstructions and illusions standing in your way back home.

The Outer World

Before proceeding to the first point of entry, which is called 'the outer world', I will refresh your memory, so you don't forget what we're up to. I will do the same refreshing again later when we proceed to our second point of entry. What needs to be refreshed here is *the angle of reentry*:

No one in your world ever needs to be forgiven,
but you are always the one who needs to forgive.

This is what you must remember every step of the way. And with 'the way', I don't mean only this book. I mean your whole life. The angle of reentry is your ticket to the highway to realization—discovering reality. If you forget it, you will not perish, but the road will be far more rough and arduous. This is one of the promises I make to you: you *will not* and *cannot* perish no matter what road you take. I only suggest you heed the message I'm here to bring and take the highway I'm presenting. The choice is yours as it has always been.

The first thing that we must cover when approaching the outer world is a desire that all sentient beings harbor. All beings in relative existence have a deep longing to be seen as they truly are. This desire drives their behavior and governs all their thoughts and deeds, but it is rarely seen by oneself or others. In fact, it is almost never seen. Forgiveness is a vehicle to that vision, and through forgiveness, you can bestow your brothers and sisters the gift of being seen as they truly are. No one else can do it but you. Now I will explain to you the mechanics of how forgiveness acts as the vehicle for fulfilling this deep human desire.

You can bestow your brothers and sisters this gift simply because you too harbor the same desire. The desire to be seen is usually not very obvious, and you are mostly not aware of it, but rest assured that it does govern all your thoughts and deeds. This desire can exist only in your interactions with your brothers and sisters—who express the same level of form and consciousness with you. You and your brothers and sisters are the reasons why the element of harmony called *forgiveness* exists in the first place.

Whatever you witness your brothers and sisters do, or whatever you might think that they think, or whatever emotions you feel in them, is a product of your inherent connection to them. The connection is so deep that the way you perceive others, so will you too become. This means that your perception of your brothers and sisters will affect *you* also. It is almost needless to say that by this guideline, I advise that you think only the highest thoughts about *every single* human being you encounter.

Now, don't be confused because previously I've advised you to stop thinking, and now I tell you just the opposite. There is a place for thinking in existence because of the simple fact that thinking occurs. That place is the moment when thinking acts as the catalyst for seeing others as who they truly are. Thinking is a tool to fulfill this desire that every sentient being carries within. Thinking is an expression of perception.

Your form in this relative existence is a product of how you perceive others. There's practically no reason at all to perceive others less than what they truly are— expressions of eternity, just like you are. However, if you think less of others, you will deny yourself the eternity in you, and cast yourself in the deep oceans of confusion and sufferings of time. This is a statement that needs more emphasis here and now:

The self-image you hold for yourself can be only as high as you think of anyone else.

If you hold low thoughts—fear, judgment, criticism, jealousy, or any kind of negativity at all—of any of your brothers and sisters, you will experience yourself only as high a being as your thoughts describe. Don't be fooled by the attempts of your ego to create reflections of a better you in comparison to someone else. Whatever comparison you create between yourself and others is a product of separation, and therefore does not exist. You are not better than anyone else. Your human dignity is not greater than anyone else's. I don't mean to put you down in any way saying this, but I say it lovingly and compassionately. Your value as a human being is not in any way greater than anyone else's because human dignity and human value do not even exist since they are based on comparing.

Whenever you think less than the highest possible thought of your brothers and sisters, you drink poison you created yourself, and choke on the dust of your self-made illusions. These poison and dust seem to express something that happens in the outer world—some circumstance or another human being, for example—but they affect *you and only you*. The negativity you see around you is your own poison, which will slowly derogate the potency of your soul. The people who seem to be plain wrong, are just dust in the winds of your own mind. Don't be afraid of my choice of words even they might sound a bit harsh. The words are here to guide you back home, and sometimes harshness is a needed ingredient to help you perceive life correctly.

Let me backtrack a few sentences at this point, and ask a question on your behalf: "What is the highest possible thought of someone else?" I will assist you also in answering this important question. The highest possible thought is something that transcends the conventional ways of thinking. So, don't settle for thinking the highest possible thought in human terms and the vocabulary you've accumulated. Maybe the highest possible thought in your vocabulary is something like "a saint, benefactor, leader, God, omnipotent, creator, Universe, consciousness," or anything like that. But such simple words are not even near to the highest possible thoughts I'm leading you to find. I will reveal you a secret now, that you might not have understood ever before: your thoughts are fundamentally unlimited and formless. To understand this more clearly, let us enjoy the company of the little soul for a while.

The little soul looked at the forms through the eyes of other forms. The sense of deep peace and primordial mystery had emerged when the little soul started to become aware of the sense of separation. Every form in existence seemed separated from one another, and they perceived everything around them through the lenses they carried within.

The lenses of perception seemed very vivid, and their whispering was so intense that the little soul many times fell into their endless webs of comparison—lesser thoughts. But the sense of separation remained painfully strong, and always when the little soul emerged back from the webs of lesser thoughts, it became more aware of the separation. As the sense of separation grew more evident, so too did the experience of the little soul itself as the witness of the separation.

The little soul saw that all the lesser thoughts that seemed to govern how the forms behaved were but lifeless symbols of reality. Their own limitedness bound them in the

So, don't treat the idea of higher thoughts through your cherished ability of lesser thoughts. Higher thoughts are not symbolic—they do *not* appear in the form of words, numbers, or images. From the standpoint of the higher thoughts, it is practically insane to introduce something like the ability to compare things with each other. Higher thoughts are expressions of what you call unconditional love, openness, acceptance, and gratitude. Anything less is insanity. Being insane is not what we want, so pay attention now.

The difference between lesser and higher thoughts is very clear, and because the topic is highly important, I will make it even more clear with an example you understand easily. Because of the happenings in our personal and humanity's past, we all know the experience of physical pain. We also know war, and what it's like to be wounded. Now, imagine that someone has shot an arrow through your shoulder. It is very painful, and the arrow significantly reduces your ability of living your life. You need the arrow removed to continue whatever you were doing.

For the higher thoughts, getting rid of the arrow is the only concern because it is causing you pain now and suffering in the long run. Your vision is in a moment, where suffering has ceased completely, and all your actions in the present moment reflect that vision. Also, you acknowledge that you have become a lot wiser on how to dodge the next arrow. There are no questions asked with the higher thoughts because the situation needs no rational thinking, but simply actions that will heal you. With higher thoughts, you are at peace, even though some physical or emotional pain is present.

For lesser thoughts, getting rid of the arrow is secondary. The lesser thoughts' primary concern is a bunch of questions that need answers sooner than later: Who shot the arrow? Why was it shot in the first place? Why was the arrow shot at you, particularly? Could you have done something to evade the situation? How will you retribute the one who shot the arrow? The lesser thoughts delay your release from the pain, and when enough pain accumulates in time, suffering will appear. The lesser thoughts make you a slave to reasons and meanings that your mind has crafted out of thin air. You would be wise not to trust what is not real.

To play even more with the arrow analogy, I would have you understand that the lesser thoughts are an arrow that has pierced your flesh. Removing the arrow should be your main priority—your *only* priority. Do not cling to the reasons and meanings the arrow and the pain produce, but simply seek to get rid of them. It is easy because whenever you are ready to be healed, the medic will appear. And this medic speaks only the language of higher thoughts.

I forgive you for exercising lesser thoughts. This means that the very moment when you find yourself thinking less of others than who they truly are is the moment forgiveness emerges. It emerges because *you* need it and have summoned it for your own use. Forgiveness is your bridge to higher thoughts. You will find it very difficult to find the higher thoughts about the outer world if you are not stopped—in other words, if you're labeling, judging, and comparing through the lenses of your lesser thoughts. You will miss the presence of forgiveness if you blindly embrace the lesser thoughts in you. So, to be aware of the presence of forgiveness, *you* must be present. You must be entirely aware of the situation—whatever *is* here and now.

The outer world and the timeless present moment is your mirror, in which you look at reflections of yourself. Don't look through your egoistic intentions and desires, lest the bleak and black mirrors of your ego devour the present moment. And be careful because the ego is a master of disguise, and its intentions are many times clouded by beautiful things that might appear as love, altruism, or selflessness, for instance. Also, whenever the idea of time distorts the reflections, you know that the ego's lesser thoughts are at play. Do not give yourself time, but if you feel there must be time, approach it through your ability to exercise higher thoughts. Do not compare, judge, label, or criticize anything in your perception.

Time seems to be an intrinsic attribute of the outer world. When you perceive the outer world, you cannot but perceive the effects of time. I just said 'effects of time' because you cannot perceive time itself. And why is that? Because time itself doesn't exist. I am using very literal words here, and you should know there is no space for any kind of philosophy when I'm talking about time. When I say that time does not exist, I mean that. And to give the statement the emphasis it deserves, I will put it clearly visible here:

Time does not exist.

Only the effects of something called 'time' exist. Time is like a criminal who is never caught but is constantly committing crimes. You can find evidence of those crimes everywhere you look—things change, something is always born, and something always dies—but the criminal has already left the crime scene. This evidence, in other words, your perception of time, is an occurrence in the present moment, mostly made of lesser thoughts. Sure, it is evident that things happen, but they do not happen in time. Things happening is a cosmic play of countless interactions, which have nothing to do with 'time'. Every single one of those interactions appears in the present moment because there is nothing else than the present moment—a moment of eternity.

Now, you might think that I'm splitting hairs talking about time. I am, but each of those hairs is a crucial part of the message I bring. I assure you that as long as you give yourself time—when you derive your perception of the outer world from your memories or expectations—you will not hear the message. When you don't hear the message, you are not aware of the presence of forgiveness. And when you're not aware of forgiveness, you're not aware of the peace and harmony, which are the substance of life. This is not what we want, so pay close attention to what I will say next.

Since time does not exist, forgiveness has nothing to do with time. If you feel someone or something in the outer world needs to be forgiven, but simultaneously you feel it is not a good 'time' yet, you will delay your journey back home. Any delay will postpone your experiences of peace and harmony. Your ability to forgive does not rely on conditions or requirements. Once again, this is a statement that deserves emphasis:

There are no requirements for forgiveness to take place.

Either you embrace forgiveness now, regardless of what has happened, or you remain unaware of its presence. And I suggest that you embrace it without delay, for the sake of us both. Remember our *angle of reentry*? You never forgive someone else because they need your forgiveness. You always forgive because *you* need it to heal *yourself*. And when you're healed, you have produced the potential to step in from the hallway of our home.

I will be there all the way to witness your process of healing. I will follow you with endless compassion during every step of the way into our home. And I will do it lovingly for the simple reason that I forgive you. No conditions. Just plain forgiveness now and in eternity. However, being the fisherman who will set you free after you get a glimpse of reality above the surface, I *cannot* and *will not* force you to step in the hallway in the first place. I love you too much to exercise any force on you. I have invited you, and the invitation is heard when you leave all your lesser thoughts aside, when you treat the outer world only through higher thoughts and through the living and loving emptiness within you.

Now, it's 'time' to present a short analogy, which will clear the air of confusion that your rational mind might have produced while reading the last pages. If your mind is full of thoughts right now, I advise you again to stop. Become the present moment.

Then, imagine that life is a road. This road is very diverse—it includes some terrible, bumpy, and winding parts, as well as perfectly paved highways. Let's do this with an analogy from history because history is prone the bear nostalgy and warm memories. So, instead of a car, you will travel this road on a wooden wagon. The wagon is old—much older than you. It squeaks and clatters, but through some miraculous work of engineering, it holds together, carrying you to the distant lands.

The road is what it is. You can do nothing but accept the forms of the road. Sometimes it is arduous, and occasionally traveling on it feels effortless. There is no maintenance who you could call because the maintenance has decided that this particular road is already perfect, and whatever is perfect must not be changed in any way. However, what you have power over is the wagon you're traveling in. The wheels of the wagon determine how smooth the ride is.

The wheels are shaped according to two things: your state of acceptance and your state of resistance. These states are reflections on how you perceive the part of the road on which you are traveling right now. With resistance, the wheels will grow deformed, and even the highway feels bumpy and stressful. With acceptance, the wheels are shaped as perfect circles and are equipped with state of the art shock absorbers, so that even the bumpiest parts of the road feel nice and effortless.

In acceptance, there is no need to change anything because you are already racing toward home. Even if you didn't know anything I've told you in this book, acceptance would make your journey easy, peaceful, and harmonious. Happiness and joy will follow acceptance. However, in resistance, your journey toward home is slow and difficult. But there is hidden beauty in all resistance.

You will find forgiveness wherever there is inner resistance.

Forgiveness will be there standing right in front of you if you are but willing to see it. Don't cling to your state of resistance, and forgiveness will blossom. And how do you recognize the state of resistance? You are in that state whenever negative thoughts or emotions are present toward yourself, the situation, or your brothers and sisters. The wagon will not fall apart no matter how much you resist, but your own makings will greatly delay your journey toward home.

When you feel resistance, don't overthink it. Lesser thoughts gravitate toward resistance, and they are prone to end up in conclusions. Whenever you end up in conclusions, the intelligence that works within you, and created the perfect road for you, will almost stop functioning. I said 'almost' because it cannot totally stop functioning. Functions of eternity cannot be stopped. They can only be overlooked.

Your beloved wagon will squeak with joy when resistance turns to acceptance. The bridge which enables this paradigm shift to happen is forgiveness. When forgiveness arises, the road becomes joyful for you, not because your requirements for atonement in the outer world have been met, but simply because your resistance does not exist anymore.

What is forgiven disappears. It becomes an echo in an empty valley, just a fading memory. And what remains, is a state of unconditional forgiveness and pure awareness—the paved highway back home.

The Inner World

If you felt it was somewhat upside down to discuss so much about thoughts while the topic was 'the outer world', then this chapter, which discusses 'the inner world', will make things more clear to you. The thoughts you perceive are indeed part of the outer world, and the inner world is something very intriguing, something that you might have never experienced consciously before. But before we proceed, I made a promise some pages ago that I would refresh your memory once again by bringing up *the angle of reentry*:

> *No one in your world ever needs to be forgiven,*
> *but you are always the one who needs to forgive.*

The angle of reentry is very, very, *very important* to keep in mind every single moment. I cannot emphasize enough of its importance. It is basically your highway back home. Nothing more, and nothing less. Trust me when I say that it means practically *everything* to you. Your forgiveness is your atonement for you and *only for you*. Forgiveness is your gift to yourself. It is the most precious gift you can ever give to yourself. When you realize that what you call 'life' is all about you—not in the egoic sense, and not in the way of lesser thoughts—you are halfway through the hallway to home.

Now, we will proceed to investigate the point of entry called the inner world. While the outer world is a world of 'time' and doing, the inner world is a world of states and being. The idea of time is not involved in the inner world because no thoughts are present there that could lead you astray. I must mention here shortly, that *you actually do not think at all*. Thinking happens to you. Thinking is an attribute of the outer world. So, don't confuse thinking with the things I will lead you through in this chapter. Lesser thoughts are light years away from the inner world. Higher thoughts are somewhat closer, but still too far to be perceived as your own thoughts.

Let's get back to the inner world from this short and necessary detour about thinking. The inner world is, as I said, a world of states and being, or to be even more precise, a world of *states of being*. The 'state of being' as a description might lead you a bit astray, and in the inner world, when you are even a tiny bit astray, you are *totally* astray. This statement is equivalent to my words before: "Whenever you forget any part of yourself, you forget yourself." There are no compromises in the inner world—no grey areas. So, let me elaborate on the 'state of being' to ensure you stay on the right track.

Falling asleep is what you do quite regularly. It is your answer to the call of *the source*, the primordial nothingness in which the little soul was floating in the beginning. When you fall asleep in the evening, the content of your outer world slowly starts to fade away. Just before sleep comes and you drift into the sweet embrace of the source, there is a moment of inner emptiness. However, this emptiness does not mean that the moment is devoid of everything. It means that all content has disappeared, yet you are still fully aware and alive. In that fleeting moment, you inhabit your own state of being without any strings attached. This state of being is both the residue of your doings during the day *and* the core reason for them. Your state of being is the canvas on which you paint all your pictures. The moment you fall asleep, the canvas is very distinct in your awareness.

You usually fall asleep, experience dreams, and wake up with the same canvas within. This is because you depart and arrive at the same terminal of the primordial nothingness. Even though time seems to have moved on, nothing essential has changed. The canvas always has a basic color that underlies everything painted on it. This color affects all the pictures which you paint as an artist. If the canvas is colored with dark and dull colors, then all the artwork on it will appear negative, and if the canvas has bright and lively colors, then everything will appear positive. It is as simple as that. The canvas is your state of being—your inner world on which the images of the outer world arise. Now, you might ask: "How do I learn to change the canvas to make my life better?" It is a good question, but *not* the correct one.

Life is not about learning because, ultimately, there is nothing to learn. A more fundamental question to ask yourself would be: "What am I teaching?" In the present moment, whatever the outer world might offer you, you are teaching the state of being that you hold within. Who, then, are you teaching this? Yourself and your brothers and sisters. And how does this teaching work practically? It's quite simple and straightforward. If you are in a state of negativity—irritation, jealousy, hate, anger, anxiety, fear, guilt, apathy, despair, you name it—then you are teaching your negativity to yourself and others around you. State of positivity—love, compassion, acceptance, serenity, gratitude, joy, trust, openness, and many others—teaches you and your brothers and sisters positivity. However, don't confuse this teaching I'm talking about with a process of learning. Learning as a consequence of teaching is a thing of the outer world. The inner world has no consequences. It acknowledges only your *present state of being*, and nothing else. Now, pay attention because this is important:

To choose what to teach, you must be aware of your state of being.

In other words, you must be aware of your inner world. Awareness is your key to returning home. There are two basic kinds of awareness: spotlight awareness and floodlight awareness. Both have their place in relative existence, but you must know and experience the distinction between them.

When dealing with things in the outer world, you normally inhabit *spotlight awareness*. This means your mind wanders quite linearly from one thing to another, without being able to understand the big picture. You cherish one thought at a time, and you focus only on one thing at a time. You might have a feeling that you understand totalities and much-encompassing truths, but in reality, your understanding with spotlight awareness is next to nothing when talking about big pictures. What you understand is but separation, which usually produces only reflections of the ego. The ego's reflections do not emerge always, but spotlight awareness is prone to produce egoic behavior.

When dealing with the inner world, you always inhabit *floodlight awareness*. This awareness doesn't focus on things simply because there are no things in the inner world. There is only your state of being. Awareness of your state of being is all-encompassing, and *all* things in the outer world include in it. With the floodlight awareness, you will find out that there cannot be thoughts—neither lesser or higher ones—without a state of being. To understand this better, you can imagine your state of being as a bowl filled with myriad things of the outer world. The bowl always has a form that determines how your life appears. This form is your state of being, and it governs everything poured into the bowl. *Spotlight awareness* is concerned only with the contents of the bowl—one thing at a time. *Floodlight awareness* is your awareness of the form of the bowl, and therefore the floodlight awareness encompasses everything in the bowl. As I said before, awareness is your key to returning home. True awareness of anything changes everything. The little soul found it out also!

The little soul played with higher thoughts. The play bestowed much joy because of the intrinsic balance of suffering and happiness the play held within. The little soul exercised lesser thoughts in one form, only to meet them with higher thoughts in another form. The dance of thoughts was beautiful, and their illusoriness in the dream-like flux called 'time' was intriguingly elusive.

Every thought emerging was always preceded by a state of being. However, all the swirling thoughts obstructed the discovery of the state of being. Time and again, the state of being was overlooked and the thoughts were the only things the little soul knew to be real. And the little soul experienced how painfully small and restricting thoughts could be. Lesser thoughts included illusions of understanding totalities, and they were proven untrue by the deepness of the higher thoughts. Even though higher thoughts felt like on the brink of revelation, their intrinsic ties to lesser thoughts made them restricted as well.

Whenever the little soul's awareness shifted toward its own essence, which happened continuously in eternity, the awareness of thoughts increased. With the awareness, some gaps in between thoughts started to emerge. The little soul discovered a whole new world behind the thoughts—a world that was preliminary for all the thoughts and forms. A world that was static and did not rely at all on the changing flux of time. The little soul found out that an absolute state of being preceded every single form in relative existence.

There were many states of being. Every time they were discovered, the sense of relativity disappeared, and all that remained was the state of being. And every time the little soul became aware of its state of being, the state of being shifted— the awareness of the state of being changed it immediately. There was no experience of time involved in that change. All that existed was an absolute state of being intrinsically connected to the awareness.

There was something peculiar in the way the states of being changed. The change always seemed to happen in the same way, ending up in the same perception of it. The little soul felt the state of being shift whenever it perceived some form as the form really was through the perspective of another form. This natural meeting of forms brought up appreciation and acceptance. Ultimately, expressions of something called love emerged.

Now we're ready to proceed to the topic of 'how your state of being changes'. Remember that we all want to be seen as who we really are, and we want to be loved for who we are. To live this way, simply try to see your brothers and sisters as who they really are and love them without conditions. This doesn't seem a very rational way because the human mind is filled with delusional conclusions about other people, and it loves invariably *with* conditions. When I talk about the 'human mind', I mean your mind, and my mind, and all the individual and collective minds we all have established. To choose the road of true vision and unconditional loving is literally *a road less traveled*, but it is the only road you have which will lead you back home.

When you're aware of your state of being, which can only be discovered through the floodlight awareness, you will have but one choice: to honor and appreciate your own state of being as it is. Be careful not to include any sense of morality or other lesser thoughts when choosing to appreciate your state of being because such are only apparitions of the outer world, and are likely to produce only separation and ultimately inhuman behavior. Just welcome your state of being as it is and observe it without judgment and valuing. You will find out that the act of sincere observation will do the trick of changing your state of being. Once again, an important thing to highlight:

You are not the one that changes your state of being.
It changes as a result of your awareness.

You *do not* and *cannot* change your state of being. You can only observe how your state of being turns out, and it changes through the simple act of observation. And here comes a huge spoiler: if you are really, sincerely, and deeply aware, there is only one state of being to turn out.

It is your essential state of being that is produced as a direct expression of *the source*. Your only true state of being is openness—the acceptance of everything the world paints on your canvas. And to be more accurate, it is the acceptance of everything your brothers and sisters paint on *your* canvas. *Love them without conditions.* All the other states of being are but illusions of the ego, which we will discuss soon. Just one addition to becoming aware of the state of being before that.

If you cannot find your state of being—meaning that you encounter only emptiness in the gaps between your thoughts—then your inner world is in coherence with the primordial nothingness. The waves of this coherence bring you very close to the source, and the brink of remembering home and who you are. There cannot be a desire to change your state of being at all if you cannot find it, but only a desire to be still and wait for the unity to happen. I will elaborate on *the lesson of unity* after dealing with the concept of the ego, which we will do next.

A word of warning is convenient here. Knowing and experiencing the different levels of awareness—the spotlight and the floodlight awareness—in yourself has nothing to do with mental or spiritual superiority. Your spiritual evolution can happen only in time, and as you must already know, time does not exist. Therefore, your spiritual evolution does not exist. It is merely another illusion of the ego. In the inner world, there's nowhere to go to, and nothing to achieve. There is only your state of being now and forever. However, there is a catch, which is called *the ego*.

I cannot let the message I bring fall in the hands of the ego. That is not what we want. The danger of that happening is highly probable, so you would be wise to stop after the following part of the book before proceeding to *the lesson of unity*. Then read this particular part concerning the ego once or twice again, so you understand what the words really mean. Then put this book down for a while—some days, or even weeks, and seek to find out what the words *really mean in your life*. Do not proceed reading this book before you've relentlessly sought the ego in your life. Only after doing so, are you wise enough to proceed to *the lesson of unity*. I cannot emphasize enough at this point, that if you're not aware of *the ego in your life*, then it will literally hijack *the lesson of unity*, and then the lesson will bring you suffering instead of liberation. Now, let us begin the investigation of the ego.

The ego is a symbol of separation. It is a layer in between the inner world and the outer world, which distorts and confuses your ability to perceive things as they are. The ego distorts reality. The reason I bring it up in the chapter concerning the inner world is that your awareness of the inner world seems most affected by the ego. Remember, though, that the inner world *is not* and *cannot* be affected by the ego, but only *your awareness* of the inner world can be.

The ego is a master of lesser thoughts, and it thrives on the conflicts that lesser thoughts are prone to produce.

Your unconscious belief in the existence of the ego keeps it alive, and consequently, *you* are likely to perceive and experience conflicts around you. It is your own belief in the ego that makes you blind to your state of being and casts you into the deep oceans of oblivion—into the myriad forms and thoughts of the outer world. The ego lies to you, promising that liberation can be attained through the outer world.

The ego seeks to blind others to hide its own blindness. Forms are all that exist in the ego's realm, but even the forms are not perceived as they are through the ego. You will find out that the ego's existence is dark and sad when you know and experience it in your own life. It is chained forever in the confusion of forms and delusional states of being, and any state of being that is delusional cannot exist. The ego's life is all about struggling to exist and to survive. This is why it experiences quite much everything as a threat to itself. When the ego feels threatened, it seeks to prove to itself that it exists. Hence the conflicts and confusion.

The ego is created out of fear. To be more precise, you give it birth when you're afraid of yourself. And what does it mean to be afraid of yourself? You fear your inner world—your own state of being. Through this fear, the ego holds you in its cold embrace. Through this fear, the ego becomes a vehicle for the attack, which you use to cause suffering on yourself as well as your brothers and sisters. The reflections in the dark mirror of the ego make you believe that *you* can be threatened, and usually, the threat delusionally seems to take forms of your brothers and sisters. This is why you attack them, sometimes with words, or when things break really bad, with physical attacks.

The ego is blind in its attacks, and it seeks to draw others into the same blindness to prove only that the ego exists. So, the ego is in existential crisis all the time, and nothing can awaken it from that delusional state of being—literally *nothing*. This kind of a confused entity we're talking about, and there is one inside every single human being.

Unlike what you've learned so far, there are no levels of power of the ego. There are no bigger or smaller egos, but the ego simply *is*. This is because it is a symbol of separation that distorts and confuses your awareness of your state of being, and as you already know, the state of being simply *is*. As I said, the ego is in all of us. There's one within me and inside all your brothers and sisters. The ego is also within *you*.

"What?" you might ask. "Preposterous! I don't have anything so dark and sad within me!" you might think. But be warned: whenever you try to fight the ego, or actively deny its existence in you, you become the ego. Whenever a thought "I have no ego" arises, it means the ego is in control. Let me clarify my preposterous statement with as practical description as I can:

The ego is your identification with thoughts.

When you blindly believe your own thoughts, and the meanings those thoughts create, then you're dealing with the ego. It might be that sometimes the ego appears happy and exuberant, but since it lives on lesser thoughts, there is conflict hidden deep within it. If you really examined thoughts, especially lesser thoughts, you would find out their conflicting nature. Lesser thoughts are symbols of resistance of what is.

The ego is full of moral codes and values. However, the moral codes of the ego are but lifeless symbols of real values that the inner world and the outer world hold within. Simply put, if you believe that your moral codes and your values are right, and you cherish them like hell, the ego is in control. However, this control is not very evident. The ego is elusive. You cannot find it when you look for it, but it will leave piles of lifeless bodies and barren land in its wake. When you derive your identity from your thoughts, your wake might not seem so dark *to you*, but this is because you believe in the ego's concepts of right and wrong. The ego always goes to war for righteousness, and all righteous wars have their victims.

Everything I'm telling you can feel a bit dark. But stay with me. I assure you that if you don't acknowledge this darkness in you, it will devour you. And when time happens to you, it will cause you much suffering. As long as you're not aware of your own blindness, healing can never occur. Without healing, darkness will prevail. The little soul also found this dark place I'm leading you through.

The expressions of love came and went, and the little soul enjoyed the wave-like nature of it all. However, the experiences of love withheld something that was not love. The greater the experience of love was, the bigger the fear of losing it grew. The greatest love that the little soul could feel was love for itself, expressed through all the forms in the relative existence. This love was so vast and all-encompassing that it created the deepest fear the little soul could ever imagine—the fear of not existing. This fear was so powerful that it blinded the little soul and cast it into many dark places.

The little soul started feeling it was not enough in itself. There was something that needed to be done to ensure the little soul's survival. However, the little soul didn't know what needed to be done, and so the insane need for survival was disguised in many forms. Those forms felt as well, as parts of the little soul, that they were not enough. And when they were not enough, they thought they couldn't be loved. No matter how much strain the forms introduced in the relative existence, they could but create ephemeral sensations of love. Love that was time-bound that would eventually wither away and be forgotten.

Deep within, the little soul could not understand this kind of love since its desire to expand was limitless. Along with the desire, the love that the little soul felt was also limitless. However, these experiences of temporary love cast the little soul into a deep state of confusion. Confused, the little soul felt it had to find meanings for all the love that existed—love that had to be compulsively grasped, and love that had already withered away into endless oceans of memories and oblivions.

I must lift some weight off your shoulders for just a short moment by assuring you that the darkness cannot prevail eternally. It will end by itself because of who you are. The darkness of the ego is only echoes from oblivion, which has already been atoned for you. This atonement occurs through forgiveness, and you can rest assured that you are completely and unconditionally forgiven. But let's get back to investigating the ego. We're almost through this.

Inner peace is your nature. Conditioned inner peace is the ego's nature. This means that the ego can know peace only if certain requirements, consisting of lesser thoughts, are met. If the requirements are not met, the ego's dark reflections will produce suffering. So, the ego is not totally devoid of peace and goodness. Some peace and goodness arise in it because it is born out of *your* belief, but its dark reflections make it so that the ego can never perceive *only* peace and goodness. This is because the ego analyzes, segregates, and divides all forms, as well as the form of itself.

There are many forms of the ego that your brothers and sisters carry within. Let us travel back to the pond analogy—which I told you before as preliminary information for *the lesson of unity*—to make the forms of the ego more clear to you. Now, the rain is pouring down from the heavens. Countless waterdrops race downward to meet the surface of the pond. When they hit the surface, the impact creates expanding patterns of waves—small waves, big waves, and waves of every size in between. It is important to understand here that the differences between the physical sizes of the waves do not matter at all. What we must focus on is the interactions between the waves.

The small waves acknowledge that they are small, and the big waves know that they are big. The small waves are fearful and withdrawing because of their situation. "I hope the big waves do not rush over me. If I just stay small and invisible, they won't see me. But if I just go with the flow, maybe the big waves will look favorably upon me and let me race with them." they think. Correspondingly, the big waves' thoughts are: "Here I am! See me and my accomplishments! I will rush over you, and I will do it with force, but if you succumb, I might look favorably upon you. Maybe we will merge and create something even bigger!"

The small waves and the big waves are always dependent on each other. The waves need something to compare themselves to. Without all kinds of waves, an individual wave would not be able to define itself. A small wave feels small because of the response it gains through the interactions with the bigger waves. A big wave feels big because small waves exist. They are all dependent on each other.

The ego breathes in the interactions of the waves, regardless of their physical size. I said this to you earlier in other words: "there are no levels of power of the ego". There are many forms of the ego, of which none are different from each other in behavior. The ego is simply a state of identifying with your thoughts, and nothing else. It can never become anything else because of its intrinsic dependence on time.

Time is the playground of the ego. The ego needs the future to fulfill itself and the past to understand itself. In the constant loop of becoming, it simultaneously tries to get away from itself and catch itself. This play with the idea of time exiles the ego from the present moment—the only moment there is. The ego's own blindness prevents it from seeing the present moment, and this is why the ego is insane.

Remember how I've told you that time does not exist? Anything that is not in the present moment does not exist. Simply because time doesn't exist, and the ego's playground is time only, this means that the ego does not exist—only *your belief* in the ego does. So, I invoke your wisdom not to exile yourself from the present moment by believing in the ego. When you relinquish your belief, the ego will be no more. You have all the tools now and forever to liberate yourself.

I forgive you for repeatedly, completely, and utterly forgetting your inner world, and projecting it through the dark reflections of the ego into the outer world. This delusional projection is not what we want. So, relentlessly try to find your true state of being. Do not believe in delusional states of being that have strings of forms and time attached to them. Go within. Deep within. Question every thought that arises, both lesser and higher thoughts. With enough awareness, your true state of being will arise by itself. Awareness expels all the confusion of the belief in the ego.

Remember this: your state of being can be quite much anything spanning from positive to negative. Do not try to change your state of being. Any effort to change it always happens in the illusion of time and the ego. Simply become aware of your state of being. This is what you call 'being true to yourself'. With sincere and natural awareness, you bestow yourself the gift of seeing yourself as you are. This gift is also yours to give to your brothers and sisters, without limits. This is what is so miraculous about you, what the ego can never understand. The truth will set you free. The truth will open your eyes to *the lesson of unity*.

And now, as I warned you before, you must soon stop reading this book. Maybe for a couple of days, weeks, months, or however long it might take for you to find out what it really means to identify with your thoughts. The unconscious belief in the ego is in you, no matter how egoless you might feel at times. Your thought of denying your ego might be the first hint of it. Now, I will not leave you alone and empty-handed on your attempts to reveal the ego.

I am inclined to give you a tool, a short and straightforward tool: *watch the gaps in between your thoughts*. Watch them closely. And in those gaps, reflect three things. *First*, do you feel you were present or absent when the last stream of thought was pouring? If you feel you were absent, then the ego was in charge. Do not overthink this, but simply observe how you feel about it. *Second*, in the gaps between the thoughts, observe your inner world—your state of being. Simply become aware of the undercurrent of the present moment, and just let it be as it is. *Third*, just sit back and wait eagerly what your next thought will be. And here comes a spoiler for this last one: as long as you are truly alert, there will *not* be a next thought. If the next thought appears without your clear decision to have that thought, then you will have become absent, and the ego is in control again.

So, have fun doing the inner detective work. Remember to keep it nice and not too grave—you must *not* try to banish the ego, lest you become the ego yourself. Just become aware of it. You will know when this work is through. And once more, heed my advice:

Do not proceed reading this book before you've relentlessly sought the ego in your life.

The Lesson of Unity

Beloved. We have journeyed some distance together now, and things are about to get serious. Not like 'you must frown while you read' serious, but 'sincerely and without any heaviness' serious. This seriousness is not based on empty intellectual or moral codes but precedes all intellect and morals. This statement carries us straight to the core of *the lesson of unity*:

Enlightenment is not a state of intellectual understanding.

Now, here is a word that is possibly one of the most inflated words ever invented. There are so many meanings attached to 'enlightenment' that all other words would grow pale next to it if words had color. Let us not be distracted by the meanings and the whispers from the past, and let us investigate what the core statement of *the lesson of unity* means.

First, you must understand what I've told you earlier in this book about words. You must be able to see the words only as pointers to what we're dealing with here. Words *do not* and *cannot* carry any truth within them. They are lifeless conveyors of life, so don't cling to any words or meanings of words, unless you want to become lifeless yourself. Words are nothing more than expressions of lesser thoughts. When we talk about 'enlightenment', the word is a signpost pointing to the huge mountain rising right next to it. Despite there is no distance between the signpost and the mountain, when you stare at the signpost, you become blind to the mountain. Do not trust words. Do not repeat any words which you have heard about enlightenment, not even the words in this book. No one can tell you what enlightenment is. The purpose of *the lesson of unity* is to remove obstacles so that you can find it out yourself. No one else can show you the way but *you*.

When you relax and become open for any thought to emerge—in fact, you can do so right now because this doesn't need any intellectual contemplation—all thoughts cease to happen. This simple observation is evidence that all thoughts are a form of resistance, and force is needed to exercise them. When you do not apply any force, then your thoughts will be no more. Sounds simple, doesn't it? And how liberating it is not to dwell in thoughts, especially leaving behind all the lesser thoughts on which the ego thrives. This experience of liberation is your shining mountain, and your first step toward *unity*. Seek for the mountain, and even a small glimpse of it in the distant horizon will prepare your understanding of the unity.

I have told you before about your journey back home. The journey that carries you in a perfect angle through the two points of entry—the outer world and the inner world. This is a perfect place to describe the journey in a bit more detail, though highly metaphorically. The description starts with a curious statement: *from the hallway to the heart of your home, there is no door.* There never was, and never will be. This is why some mystics have called it the doorless door, the gateless gate.

Now, I will make one of my deepest promises to you. I stand in the hallway of your home *eternally*, pointing you the way. If you happen to overlook me and don't listen to my loving words, I will spend an eternity waiting for you here. From here, the doorless door is not any distance away, but passing through is literally *a journey without a distance.* There is no need to delay this journey. If you delay this journey, you delay your own healing. The only thing insane enough to delay one's own healing is the ego. More precisely, your belief in the existence of the ego will stand in your way of healing. Overcoming any delay is not an act of intellect or willpower, but an act of desire.

Remember, when I told you about your deepest and first desire? The desire to expand. Enlightenment is a metaphor for the realization that wherever and whenever you're standing right now, you're standing in the hallway of your home, and from there you can expand without limits. This boundless capability of expansion is possible because there is no door to pass through. It simply happens that your first point of expansion is your home. Enlightenment whispers wordless words that your home is also your last point of expansion. There's nowhere to go to and nothing to do. Is it so hard to believe? It might be, but I assure you that *you never left home.* You just happened to forget that you were standing there all the time—in the hallway in which no door separates you from the heart of your home. To remember this is unity. To experience this is peace.

You might wonder now that how do you attain this unity and this peace? As I've told you before, the elements of harmony were created solely for this purpose, and the shiniest of them is forgiveness. Forgiveness is a bridge that shows you out from your delusional way of living and guides you back home. The angle of reentry must be *perfect,* so here it comes once again:

No one in your world ever needs to be forgiven,
but you are always the one who needs to forgive.

You must understand that you are the only one that needs forgiveness to happen. If you don't understand this, then all your efforts in forgiving will be subject to exercising force. As you already know, force means resistance, and resistance carries you further away from the shining mountain of enlightenment—back into the lightless valleys of the ego. This is not what we want. Forgiveness, when applied perfectly in the angle of reentry, is natural to you and does not require any force at all.

Forgiveness is not an act of forgiving what someone else or you have done. It is the realization that what someone else or you did has not taken place at all. True forgiveness undoes everything that needs to be forgiven, just like the rising sun in the spring melts away all the trails in the snow. When the trails become nothing, you are liberated. Memories of those trails might remain, but you are not destined to walk on them anymore.

When you forgive your brothers and sisters, it is *you* who will be set free. It is *you* who will be healed. It is *you* who will be whole. This is the state of being that you teach through forgiveness. This enlightened state of being—where you are free, healed, and whole—is just prior to your act of expanding into your home. And you are free, healed, and whole whenever you're empty of all thoughts of the outer world. You have left the outer world devoid of *all* meanings. And you will leave the inner world meaningless also when you realize what *the lesson of unity* is all about.

In truth, there's no distinction between the outer world and the inner world. Existence *is* only as a whole. As I said earlier, the two points of entry are separated in this book only because of teaching purposes. The divisive nature of the mind and language binds me to present this distinction in a dualistic way. This dualism is the fishing rod that I use to lift you above the surface so that you can see the truth. Then, you can make your own decisions about what you desire to do. I have gone through many obstacles and definitions with you simply to give you the tools to decide wisely. Remember this:

There is no wisdom in lesser thoughts,
very little in higher thoughts,
some in states of being,
and all wisdom in forgiveness.

Forgiveness heals—first you and then your brothers and sisters—and as a consequence of healing, it unites. *The lesson of unity* dismantles the illusion of the armor of separation that you have crafted around you. The armor itself cannot be dismantled because it is just an illusion; the armor does not even exist. So, only the illusion can be dismantled. You might have noticed that we're talking about the ego here—the symbol of separation. Separation is a product of your imagination, your expansion into the world of lesser thoughts, the idea of time, and the ego.

Unity is everything but separation, in the same way that enlightenment is the end of suffering. There are no definite descriptions for them, but only the realization of what they are *not*. Unity is the all-encompassing little soul looking at one form through the eyes of another form. It is the experience of the little soul when it realizes its own nature after the oblivion of forms.

After countless eons of confusion and insanity in the relative experience of time, the forms started shifting. Slowly, but steadily they opened to something they did not understand at first, yet what felt familiar and loving in a peculiar way. The essential nature of the little soul was beginning to blossom through the forms. As that happened, the little soul's remembrance of itself grew deeper.

Tiny sparks of remembrance flashed here and there among the forms, like stars that shined for their time in the embracing darkness of space. Every time the remembrance happened, the little soul's wordless knowledge of itself grew deeper. And the deeper the knowledge was, the more expanding was the conscious presence of the little soul among the forms. Whenever the forms felt the presence, even for a fleeting moment in time, they knew they were loved, that they were enough. They understood that nothing needed to be atoned anymore— everything was forgiven. The forms knew they were already home.

Endless times in separation were coming to an end. The forms that once felt separate from each other started to gradually understand that they intrinsically connected through the simplest and most beautiful thing in existence: the One which encompassed everything with unimaginable power, yet which flowed through the forms silently like valley streams through the mountain range. The One that had expanded into every single form in the relative existence.

The little soul smiled lovingly within all forms for its own misplaced expansion into oblivion, insanity, and confusion. Through the awakening of the forms, it realized that the relative existence had been but a dream being dreamt within eternity. Despite being just a dream, it was not a meaningless dream. It fulfilled the little soul's deepest desire to expand. As the result of the expansion, the little soul realized who it was.

Over and over again, the realization happened. Over and over again, the expansion occurred, resulting in the realization. Primordial love and joy were found time and again, though 'time' played no part at all in it. The process of the little soul was eternal, devoid of time, and empty of all meanings. The little soul was eternally unified, and the peaceful state of not knowing fluctuated within and without.

Everything is one. One is everything. Whatever world you might perceive outside of you, is actually within you. All the fear the ego carries is in *you*, and any experience of attack by your brothers and sisters against you happen within *you*. Also, all the love you're able to share—the unlimited love and openness, which isn't exercised through force and does not introduce any strain to your being—happens within you. You can share love only from yourself to yourself. Whatever projections this sharing might produce in the outer world, reflect *you*.

Is this all hard to accept? Believe me, when the illusion of the ego's armor has been dismantled, you don't even have to accept this. It becomes evident that the world is within you, and what is evident does not need conscious acceptance. I must caution that I'm not describing the 'you' that you think about, care about, or feel about. I'm not talking about 'you' as an accumulation in time. That's all separation. I'm describing *you as the little soul.*

Remember when I used the spacecraft analogy to introduce you to the angle of reentry and the points of entry? Let us dive back into that for just a short moment. Now, you want to get back home from your space odyssey. Your navigation is accurate, and your angle of reentry is perfect. You soar through the points of entry—the outer world and the inner world—and arrive home. Joy, unlike any other, fills your soul and soothes your strained mind. Peace starts to pour in, not from any outside place, but from within you. This peace has no opposite, and therefore it cannot break. It was never born, so it cannot die. It never began, so it will never end. It was never created, so it can never be destroyed. You just feel joyful and peaceful for no reason whatsoever. This peace is your essential nature— the primordial stillness.

In this stillness, you perceive your past journey back home in a totally different way. Your journey through the points of entry had ultimately been a journey through yourself—a journey without a distance. You *understand* and *experience* that you never actually left home. You just happened to follow the desire to expand deeper into yourself, and this expansion happened to create a whole lot of different forms and states of being. While the expansion was occurring, you stood immovable at your home, watching curiously through the doorless door how the forms arose and fell like the waves in an ocean. With this peaceful inner vision, you realize that the play of appearance and disappearance of the relative existence— the play of hide and seek—deserves your unconditional forgiveness. This forgiveness heals you and all your brothers and sisters who are forms of you.

I know this all might sound a bit sappy and a bit too abstract, but as I've said a few times before, I must use words to do this here. Words cannot do miracles, but words can point to miracles. Just because of courtesy, I will get down to the ground and offer you a simpler, less abstract description of what I just told you above. Here it comes.

We're all on the same spinning planet that soars through the emptiness that has no end. What in the world could be a reason to feel separate from each other? What in the heavens could be a reason to quarrel and attack one another? What on Earth would be a reason not to love your brothers and sisters as yourself? There is *none* because we intrinsically connect as organisms on this vaster organism called Earth. We also inherently connect through the attribute of simply existing. It is an expression of insanity that we feel separate from each other. Insanity can only be a symbol for what is unreal, and nothing unreal exists. Also, what is real cannot be protected because reality cannot be threatened. This is the essence of the primordial stillness. This is the message of the little soul conveyed through words that I am here to bring you.

Everything you perceive in your brothers and sisters, you perceive in *yourself*. All the highs and lows you experience with them are the high and low aspects of *you*. Everyone lives in you. You live in everyone. The eternal

One is many, and the many are One. *This is the lesson of unity.*

I Forgive You

At the beginning of our journey together, I said that I forgive you. This is my most humble promise to you. You are entirely forgiven here and now. You are loved without conditions and requirements. You are accepted without having to become anything else than what you are right now. You are perfect just as you are. I forgive you simply because *I know who you are*. Now, here are some things in particular, for which you are forgiven. There are countless others also, but these are something that will amplify the echoes of the invitation to our home—back to the remembrance and realization of the little soul.

I forgive you for treating yourself not worthy of your own love.

A virus roams in your being, distorting reality. It whispers in your mind that you are not enough and that you cannot be loved. This causes you much suffering because you long for being loved, and you believe you can achieve love only by being enough. But as long as you think such lesser thoughts, the virus prevents you from ever being enough. I assure you that you already are enough, and you already are loved. There is nothing you must do to acquire love. The whole existence loves you beyond all reason.

I forgive you for mistreating yourself.

There are many times when you treat yourself in a highly unfriendly manner, even violently one could say. If you had friends who you treated the same way, those friends would not call you a friend anymore. You would be wise to treat yourself just like you treat your dearest friend in the whole world. This is because *you* are your best friend. No more important relationship exists than your intimate relationship with yourself. Only when this relationship is healed, will all the other relationships in your outer world be healed. I promise to you that my forgiveness will heal you.

Most human life is in a vicious loop of becoming. Quite much every single human is subject to that loop, mostly without even knowing it. This continuous state of becoming chains you in the illusions of the outer world. In those chains, time will eventually present suffering. A time will come when all your capabilities of becoming will greatly deteriorate, and ultimately the becoming will cease altogether. At that moment, all your efforts of getting away from yourself stop, and you no longer strive to catch yourself. You must know that your essence is not in becoming, but in *being*. Remember this, and you will find my forgiveness.

I forgive you for ending up in conflicts with your brothers and sisters.

The ego within you thrives on conflicts. It is a machinery of pain and war. Any conflict you encounter in your daily life is a child of the ego. No matter how big or small the conflict is, it is a seed for war and widescale devastation. Do not cherish that seed, lest you exile yourself from peace. Your brothers and sisters have *nothing* to do with your inner peace, so you would be wise not to project your own inner conflicts on their responsibility. The moment you realize that all conflicts you experience are created by *you* and the insane apparatus called the ego, you will find out that those conflicts do not even exist. This is simply because the ego does not exist. This means that you are already liberated from all conflicts.

Lesser thoughts are prone to create suffering. Even if the conflicts with your brothers and sisters do not take place physically in the outer world, the conflict might still arise within you in the form of lesser thoughts. When you live through your conditioned compulsive thinking, you can often find yourself thinking disrespectfully of your brothers and sisters. It might appear like a small grain of irritation or a huge inner flame of anger and hate. This does not tell anything about your brothers and sisters, but it describes only the lesser state of being that *you* are in. It is highly important to understand that any lesser thought about anyone else will make *you* less. This does not have to be— just strive to become aware of your thinking patterns when you feel even the tiniest irritation, and you will see what my words mean. Focus on yourself instead of the others, and you will find inner peace awaiting you.

I forgive you for being afraid that time will run out.

As I said earlier, time does not exist. But your normal state of being refuses this statement. A part of you lives through time, and when living through time, the belief that time will run out automatically appears. A sense of hurry is introduced in your life. It might be hurry because of some insignificant task of the day or hurry because of all the things you believe you must achieve before you 'depart' from 'life'. In truth, there is no hurry simply because time does not exist. Things happen, and the world flows just as perfectly without a sense of hurry. There is no better place for you to be than where you are right now. Wherever you go, there you are. This is not a philosophical statement, but as literal as a statement can get. Become aware of where you are, and stay in that awareness. You will see how the world flows by itself—peacefully.

Your lesser thoughts are not important. They do not define anything important, even though they seem as if they did. As you know from the earlier part of this book, lesser thoughts are symbols made of words, images, and numbers. An inherent limitedness dwells in all symbols, of which the ego is the most limited one. As a symbol of separation, the ego consists solely of lesser thoughts, yet even them the ego cannot understand perfectly. Do not blind yourself with beliefs based on nothing. Do not let your false ideas of conflicts take over. Your life is devoid of all conflict. In your aware presence, the absence of suffering emerges. In you, formless love prevails, and so your only true vision is one of wordless acceptance, appreciation, and gratitude.

The lesser thoughts are prone to produce idols. In human life, these idols are presented in the forms of people, and sometimes gods. Existing only in your mind, all idols are but symbols based on comparing. Comparison can take place only in illusions of time and the realms of the ego. There's nothing to which you can compare yourself. No one is higher than you, greater than you, or more perfect than you. And vice versa, no one is lower than you, lesser than you, or more imperfect than you. Idols, either higher or lower ones, are but whispers in the wind. You are the atmosphere in which all winds blow.

You have grown to love your pain and suffering. If you've paid attention before, you will remember what I said about 'silent suffering'. All the conflicts in your life, and the lesser thoughts concerning your brothers and sisters, are produced by your silent suffering. And you are most probably not even aware of your state of suffering. This is why it's called silent. Don't deny your suffering, and don't overlook it, but become aware of it. The denial of suffering in you is a direct refusal to be healed. You cannot suffer without on some level being open to the presence of suffering. Only the ego is insane enough for cherishing suffering and refusing to be healed. However, you should not exile the ego and reject its suffering. That would be an unwise thing to do because when you try to resist the ego, you become the ego. When you deny the ego, you become the ego. So, just let it be. You need only stand aware at the gates of your mind, and healing will pour in.

Life in Eternity

eloved. I hope you've heard the message I came here to bring. If you still feel confused, please rest assured that you will hear it in no time. And I literally mean in *no time*. This indicates that the message echoes within you in the eternal present moment. The message has never been absent, and it never will. You will hear it when the obstructions you have set *yourself* have faded into nothingness.

However, just as I said at the beginning of this book, the message does not come in words. If it was put only in words, it would activate the lesser thought system in your mind, and you would end up resisting the message. This is not what we want. I ask that you relentlessly seek the obstructions within yourself, which block your ability of higher understanding. This way, you will start hearing the message. You will hear it everywhere around you, regardless of the situation or people that surround you.

Sometimes it might be faint, and sometimes it becomes very evident.

You are playing hide and seek with reality. But it is not you who is seeking. You are the one hiding. Reality awaits your emergence eternally, and what is eternal cannot ultimately be missed. As long as you believe you know the meanings of forms—and hide behind the delusional certainty of the ego—you cannot understand that reality will find you if you just let it. There's nothing complex about it. The end of the play does not need any intellectual contemplation. The play has already ended. Reality knows you and loves you here and now. Stop hiding, and the seeker will come to you. Stop being afraid of yourself.

In eternity, there is no fear, and everything is unknown. You cannot fear the unknown. You can fear only what you know. I encourage you become aware of what you think you know because your apparent knowledge is the basis for the ego's delusions. The act of overlooking the ego, if you let it roam free outside the radar of your awareness, will leave a crucial part of you uninvestigated. A life uninvestigated will inevitably seem threatening. When taking a closer look, nothing is threatening in life. If a thought of any threat enters your mind, raise your level of awareness, and you will see that nothing needs to be protected. Salvation will arise by itself. Miracles will emerge spontaneously.

Have you ever had the feeling that something wonderful, something miraculous is going to happen, but you don't know what it is? The feeling just occurred, and you had not the slightest idea why? Such passing moments in time were always moments when you had forgiven something or someone, maybe even yourself, and your act of forgiving had set you free. This forgiveness might not even have been a conscious act. This is what *the angle of reentry* means. It is the perfect angle for the expectation of miracles to arise. When your awareness embraces it, miracles will surely happen. The elements of harmony— among which forgiveness is the brightest star in the sky— produce miracles, and there is but one reason for the elements of harmony to exist:

The ultimate essence of love cannot be conveyed through words.

The elements of harmony are the vehicles of love. Love is eternal. This simple statement should be your cue not to confuse the love I'm talking about with the clingy and needy kind of love described by lesser thoughts. True love persists and is not born in time. Therefore, it cannot wither away in time. Any love you think you've felt that is now withered away was not love, but only dependence. So, I advise you to investigate your life in and out to find *love* instead of dependence. And here comes a spoiler for the investigation: forgiveness is the key. Forgive yourself for feeling that you cannot be loved, and then you will be healed. Yet another spoiler: if you sincerely think that you can be loved and loving *because* of your shining personality and your lovable characteristics, then you're dependent on your own self-image. Only when you forgive yourself for being dependent, will you be healed. Only when healed, can you find yourself home. And rest assured, healing will come by itself if you just let it. It's already in you.

Healing will show you the way from the hallway of your home into the heart of your home. After walking through the gateless gate, everything will remain the same, yet your perception of everything has profoundly shifted. Time does not keep you in chains anymore, and the ego is but a fading memory of a passing nightmare. The little soul awakens *in you* and realizes itself *as you*. You are the little soul that's doing the remarkable creation work. You are eternal.

Now, I promised that I would guide you to see reality yourself, like the fisherman pulling the fish out from the deep waters into a whole new world and then letting them go. The choice is now yours. I trust you to choose wisely. Who will you be to express the eternity in the relative existence you've created? How will you carry this eternity as who you are?

One more thing, and then we're through. This is important, so if you've casually daydreamt your way through this book not paying enough attention, then this will be your last and clearest point of atonement. At the beginning of this book, I said that I forgive you. I really, sincerely, and lovingly do. And for what? I forgive you for forgetting who you are. I forgive you for believing in a reality that doesn't even exist. I do not forgive you because you need my forgiveness, but because *I need to forgive*. I love you, and I need to forgive you for one reason only.

I am you.